I0815265

DISCOVERING THE UNITED STATES

Alabama

BY JOANNE MATTERN

Kids Core
An Imprint of Abdo Publishing
abdobooks.com

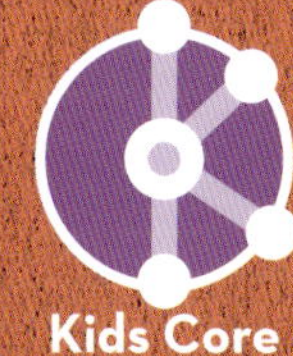

abdobooks.com

Printed in China.
052024
092024

Cover Photo: Shutterstock Images
Interior Photos: Everett Collection Historical/Alamy, 4–5; Don Cravens/The Chronicle Collection/Getty Images, 7; Fiona M. Donnelly/Shutterstock Images, 8 (top left); Ryan McGurl/iStockphoto, 8 (top right); iStockphoto, 8 (bottom left), 20–21, 26; Shutterstock Images, 8 (bottom right), 10, 17, 28 (bottom right); Giordanno Brumas/SOPA Images/Sipa USA/AP Images, 12–13; American Photo Archive/Alamy, 14; Ron Buskirk/Alamy, 15; Liam Kennedy/Bloomberg/Getty Images, 18; Danny Ye/Shutterstock Images, 22; Jon Frederick/iStockphoto, 25; Red Line Editorial, 28 (top left), 29; Shackleford Photography/iStockphoto, 28 (top right); EWY Media/Shutterstock Images, 28 (bottom left)

Editor: Christa Kelly
Series Designer: Katharine Hale

Library of Congress Control Number: 2023949219

Publisher's Cataloging-in-Publication Data

Names: Mattern, Joanne, author.
Title: Alabama / by Joanne Mattern
Description: Minneapolis, Minnesota: Abdo Publishing, 2025 | Series: Discovering the United States | Includes online resources and index.
Identifiers: ISBN 9781098293710 (lib. bdg.) | ISBN 9798384912989 (ebook)
Subjects: LCSH: U.S. states--Juvenile literature. | Alabama--History--Juvenile literature. | Southeastern States--Juvenile literature. | Physical geography--United States--Juvenile literature.
Classification: DDC 973--dc23

All population data taken from:
"Estimates of Population by Sex, Race, and Hispanic Origin: April 1, 2020 to July 1, 2022." *US Census Bureau, Population Division*, June 2023, census.gov.

CONTENTS

Rosa Parks is often called the Mother of the Civil Rights Movement.

CHAPTER 1

The Montgomery Bus Boycott

It was December 1, 1955, in Montgomery, Alabama. Rosa Parks had worked all day. Now she was on a bus, headed home.

The buses in Montgomery were **segregated**. Black passengers were forced to sit in the back of the bus.

If there weren't enough seats for white passengers, then the Black passengers had to give up their seats and stand.

When several white passengers got on, the bus driver ordered Parks to stand up. But she was tired of being treated differently than white people. Parks said "No." When she refused to move, she was arrested.

Civil rights activists in Montgomery had wanted to fight segregated buses for a long time. After Parks' arrest, they organized a **boycott**. They refused to ride the city buses until everyone had the right to sit where they wanted.

The bus boycott lasted for more than a year. Finally, in 1956, the US Supreme Court ruled that segregated buses were against the law.

During the Montgomery bus boycott, Black people walked to work or carpooled instead of riding buses.

The seats on all public buses had to be open to everyone. The people of Alabama had changed the nation.

Alabama's Land

Alabama is located in the South region of the United States. The state is bordered by Georgia to the east and Mississippi to the west. Tennessee borders Alabama to the north.

Alabama Facts

DATE OF STATEHOOD
December 14, 1819

CAPITAL
Montgomery

POPULATION
5,074,296

AREA
52,420 square miles
(135,767 sq km)

STATE BIRD

Yellowhammer

STATE TREE

Southern longleaf pine

STATE FLOWER

Camellia

STATE MAMMAL

Black bear

Each US state has a different population, size, and capital city. States also have state symbols.

Florida and the Gulf of Mexico border Alabama to the south.

Alabama has many different types of land. The north-central part of the state is home to the Appalachian Mountains. This area has high mountains, deep valleys, and rushing waterfalls. The southern part of Alabama is covered in swamps and pine forests. The Black Belt Prairie also cuts through this region. The land there is good for farming.

Alabama has beaches along the Gulf Coast. These beaches have soft white sand. There are also many rivers in Alabama. Many of these waterways drain into Mobile Bay or the Gulf of Mexico.

Alabama's Animals

Many animals live in Alabama. The forests are home to bobcats and black bears. Sea lions live on the coast. Woodpeckers and great horned owls soar across the state's skies. And rivers are home to salamanders and otters.

Alabama's state flag was adopted in 1895.

Alabama has hot summers and mild winters. It gets very little snow. However, the state gets about 56 inches (142 cm) of rain each year. It is the fourth-rainiest state in the country.

Alabama has frequent tornadoes, especially during the spring and fall. The state averages about 90 tornadoes a year. It also gets many tropical storms and hurricanes in areas near the Gulf of Mexico.

Rosa Parks explained why she refused to give up her seat:

> People always say that I didn't give up my seat because I was tired, but that isn't true. I was not tired physically. . . . No, the only tired I was, was tired of giving in.

Source: Christine Clarridge. "Remembering Rosa Parks: Words of Wisdom from 'Mother of the Civil Rights Movement.'" *Seattle Times*, 1 Dec. 2016, seattletimes.com. Accessed 28 Nov. 2023.

What's the Big Idea?

Read this quote carefully. What is its main idea? Explain how the main idea is supported by details.

The Choctaw Nation is the third-largest American Indian nation in the United States.

CHAPTER 2

The People of Alabama

The first people arrived in Alabama more than 10,000 years ago. They were American Indians. The land became home to the Chickasaw, Cherokee, Muskogee, and Choctaw nations.

French explorers settled in southern Alabama in 1702.

By the start of the American Civil War (1861–1865), more than 45 percent of Alabama's population was made up of enslaved people.

They brought enslaved people with them. The people had been kidnapped from Africa. The number of enslaved people in Alabama quickly rose. They were forced to farm and build houses.

More white **settlers** soon moved to the state, stealing American Indian land. In the 1830s, the US Army forced thousands of American Indians to leave their homes and move west. This removal is known as the Trail of Tears.

The Sacred Tears Monument honors the American Indian people who were forced to march the Trail of Tears.

As the United States expanded west, northern states wanted to stop slavery from spreading. Southern states did not. This started the American Civil War (1861–1865). In January of 1861, Alabama left the United States.

It joined a group of Southern states to start a new nation. This nation was called the Confederacy. The Confederacy lost the war. Alabama rejoined the United States in 1868.

Alabama Today

Today, almost 65 percent of people in Alabama are white. About 27 percent are Black. Nearly 5 percent are Hispanic or Latino.

Football Fans

Sports are a major part of Alabama's culture. College football is especially popular. Many people in the state are fans of the University of Alabama's football team. The team is called the Crimson Tide.

Gumbo is a West African dish that enslaved people began making in the United States.

More than 1.5 percent are Asian. Only 0.7 percent are American Indian.

Food is an important part of Alabama's culture. The state's large Black population has influenced Alabama's popular foods. Black-eyed peas, fried chicken, and a spicy stew called gumbo are dishes with roots in Black culture. These dishes are known as soul food. Other popular foods in Alabama include barbecued meats and fried green tomatoes.

Alabama's cotton industry brings in nearly $400 million each year.

Industries

Farming is an important **industry** in Alabama. Cotton is one of the state's most farmed crops. Farmers also grow foods such as corn, peanuts, and soybeans. Others raise cattle and chickens.

Many people in Alabama work in the **aerospace** industry. Several major airplane manufacturers are based in the state. Alabama is also home to the Marshall Space Flight Center. This research site develops rockets and spacecraft for the National Aeronautics and Space Administration (NASA).

Explore Online

Visit the website below. What information does it give you that was not in Chapter Two?

The American Civil War

abdocorelibrary.com/discovering-alabama

Almost 63 percent of people in Montgomery are Black.

Places in Alabama

Montgomery is the capital of Alabama. The city lies along the Alabama River in central Alabama. Montgomery was the first capital of the Confederacy during the Civil War. Today, the city has many museums, parks, and historical sites.

The US Space and Rocket Center has more than 20 rockets on display for tourists to see.

Huntsville, in northern Alabama, is the state's most **populated** city. It is home to the Marshall Space Flight Center. The center makes aerospace technology for NASA. Visitors to Marshall can see museum displays at the US Space and Rocket Center.

State Parks

Alabama has 21 state parks. One of the most popular is Cheaha State Park in eastern Alabama. It sits at the southern tip of the Appalachian Mountains. The park is surrounded by the Talladega National Forest. Visitors can climb Cheaha Mountain, the highest point in Alabama.

DeSoto State Park is in northern Alabama. It is home to DeSoto Falls, the second-highest waterfall in Alabama. DeSoto Falls is 104 feet (32 m) tall. Visitors can fish in the park's lakes.

They can hike and swim. They can ride horses. People can even go ziplining at the park!

Landmarks

The Freedom Riders National **Monument** is one of Alabama's most famous landmarks. The monument is in Anniston in eastern Alabama.

The Freedom Riders

The Freedom Riders were part of the American civil rights movement. In 1961, Black and white activists rode buses together to protest segregation. Many were threatened and beaten. But they refused to give up. In 2017, the Freedom Riders National Monument opened to honor the riders.

Visitors to DeSoto State Park can fish, kayak, hike, and rock climb.

The USS *Alabama* had a crew of 2,500 people.

It honors the Freedom Riders. They were a group of civil rights activists.

USS *Alabama* Battleship Memorial Park is another famous landmark. It is in Mobile, Alabama. The park has tanks, planes, and a submarine. It is also home to the USS *Alabama*. This battleship was used in World War II (1939–1945). Visitors can explore the ship.

Alabama is a state that is rich in history and natural beauty. People can visit historical monuments or admire the state's beautiful scenery. No matter what a person is interested in, there is plenty to explore in Alabama.

Further Evidence

Look at the website below. Does it give any new evidence to support Chapter Three?

USS *Alabama* Battleship Memorial Park

abdocorelibrary.com/discovering-alabama

State Map

KEY

Capital

Park

City or town

Point of interest

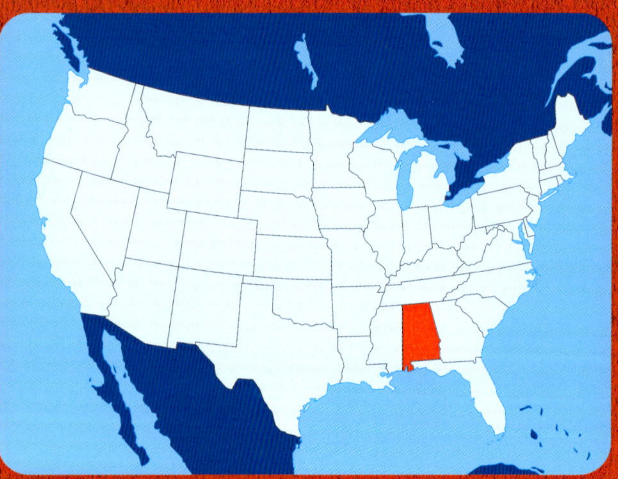

Lake Martin

Freedom Riders National Monument

Oak Mountain State Park

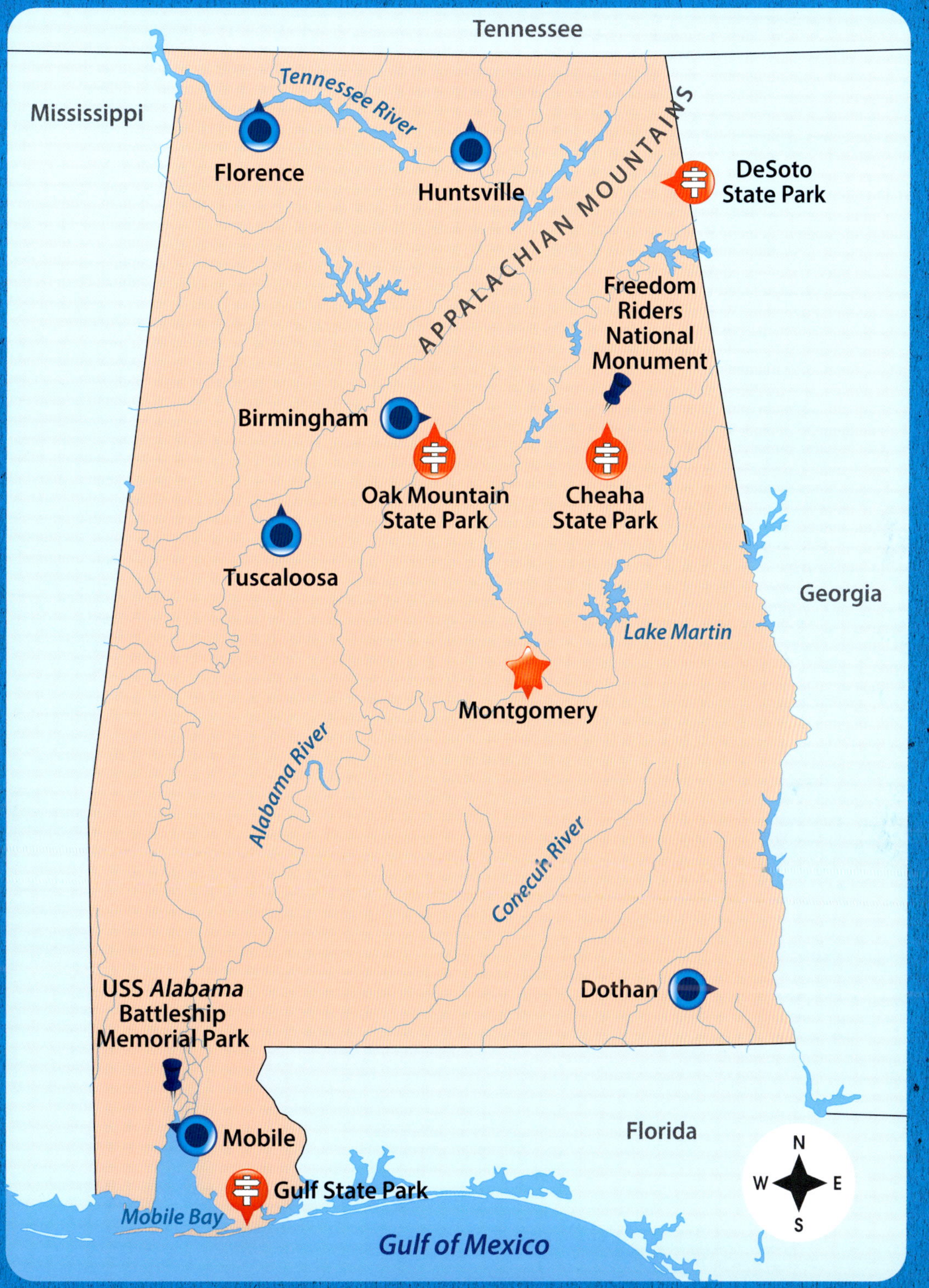
Alabama: Heart of Dixie
Tennessee
Mississippi
Tennessee River
Florence
Huntsville
APPALACHIAN MOUNTAINS
DeSoto State Park
Freedom Riders National Monument
Birmingham
Oak Mountain State Park
Cheaha State Park
Tuscaloosa
Georgia
Lake Martin
Montgomery
Alabama River
Conecuh River
Dothan
USS *Alabama* Battleship Memorial Park
Mobile
Florida
Gulf State Park
Mobile Bay
Gulf of Mexico
N
W
E
S

Glossary

aerospace
related to flight and space

boycott
a protest in which people refuse to use a specific service or buy certain goods

civil rights activists
people who fight for equal rights for minority groups

industry
a group of businesses that serve similar purposes

monument
a structure built to remind people of a person or event

populated
settled or lived in

segregated
separated by race or other characteristics

settlers
people who moved to a new area

Online Resources

To learn more about Alabama, visit our free resource websites below.

Visit **abdocorelibrary.com** or scan this QR code for free Common Core resources for teachers and students, including vetted activities, multimedia, and booklinks, for deeper subject comprehension.

Visit **abdobooklinks.com** or scan this QR code for free additional online weblinks for further learning. These links are routinely monitored and updated to provide the most current information available.

Learn More

Mallory, Shadae. *The History of the Civil Rights Movement.* Rockridge, 2021.

Parker, Philip. *The Civil War Visual Encyclopedia.* DK, 2021.

Tieck, Sarah. *Alabama.* Abdo, 2020.

Index

About the Author

Joanne Mattern is the author of many books for young readers. Her favorite topics include history, geography, biographies, and science. She loves sharing information with her readers and helping them discover new things. Mattern lives in New York with her family.